EARTH-MARKED LIKE YOU

Poems

Praise for *Earth-Marked Like You*

"Mary Dezember's new collection is enormous in scope, technical skill and experiment, and surprise. An enormous achievement. Poems like 'Skin Traveler' are sudden master poems that surprise and please: 'Your body is a map of everywhere I want to go./Yet I can see none of these places are on earth./With you, I become otherworldly,/a skin traveler...'

"Above all her precinct is love. With the variety of Sappho's solitudes, sensualities, and ironic humor, she gives us her galaxies and moon, in movement like everything on earth, before her observing and transforming eye. Read her and be transformed."

—Willis Barnstone, author of *Life Watch* and *The Restored New Testament*

"In the searching poems of *Earth-Marked Like You*, Mary Dezember tracks the vicissitudes, challenges, and triumphs of the soul trapped in a body—writing passionately of the 'memories we hide in our bodies' and 'harvested farmlands of pain,' alongside 'drifts of kindness like/Banners of snowflakes warming the sky' and the soul's ultimate freedom: 'Nakedness is not our clothes falling away,/but our bodies, our bodies flung off finally,/freeing us....' These are poems of a life's journey and hard-won knowledge."

—Carol Moldaw, author of *So Late, So Soon: New and Selected Poems* and *The Widening*

"Mary Dezember's poetry is a blend of lyrical intensity, grounded in scenes of real life. Her often startling juxtapositions raise large questions, and explore layers of different kinds of loss. Her work has a rich sense of place, beautifully and sometimes starkly set in the New Mexico landscape. In Dezember's poetry, which pushes against a 'fixed life' toward another, there is ultimately, a deep sense of hope that is uplifting."

—Diane Thiel, author of *Echolocations* and *Resistance Fantasies*

Earth-Marked Like You

Poems
Mary Dezember

SANTA FE

© 2011 by Mary Dezember
All Rights Reserved.

No part of this book may be reproduced in any form or by any electronic or mechanical means including information storage and retrieval systems without permission in writing from the publisher, except by a reviewer who may quote brief passages in a review.

Sunstone books may be purchased for educational, business, or sales promotional use. For information please write: Special Markets Department, Sunstone Press, P.O. Box 2321, Santa Fe, New Mexico 87504-2321.

Book and Cover design › Vicki Ahl
Body typeface › Bell MT
Printed on acid free paper

Library of Congress Cataloging-in-Publication Data

Dezember, Mary.
  Earth-marked like you : poems / by Mary Dezember.
       p. cm.
  ISBN 978-0-86534-852-3 (pbk. : alk. paper)
  I. Title.
  PS3604.E937E27 2013
  811'.6--dc23
                                            2011046223

WWW.SUNSTONEPRESS.COM
SUNSTONE PRESS / POST OFFICE BOX 2321 / SANTA FE, NM 87504-2321 /USA
(505) 988-4418 / ORDERS ONLY (800) 243-5644 / FAX (505) 988-1025

for
You

CONTENTS

Acknowledgements   9
Preface   13

I   At Bay

When I Had the American Dream   17
This Isn't Your Dream   18
The Truth   20
The Making of Us   22
Meadowwalk   25
At Bay   28
Heritage: The Quest to Identity by a
    Cherokee Granddaughter   30
Something Like Church or When A Woman
    Tries to Change Her Life (A Love Poem)   33
The Music of You   35

II   Transfiguration

Nocturne   41
Earth-Marked Like You   43
Rapids   45
Self-Portrait   47
The Spirit Never Sleep.s   49
Another Dead Child   51
Stigmata   54
Burning Alone   55
Conjuring You   56
Their Last Night   57
Recovery   58
Once In A Lifetime Repeatedly   59

Beyond Socorro	61
The Motion of the Night	63
A Place for the Living	65
Skin Traveler	66
Transfiguration	67
Raising a Dead Body in the Graveyard	72
Their Ears Hear Only Angels	74
Cemetery Song	76
The Second Coming	77

III New Life

It Will Be Different This Time:	85
The Healer	86
Midnight, December 25th: Divine Outlaws	89
Life Wish: The Art of Discernment	91
Shiggaion	93
Hit Me Again	96
2000 Women	97
Conscious Pilate	99
Don't Touch Me, For I Must Leave You Again, This Time, Forever	101
The Chosen	103
Nakedness	105
Frozen Music	106
Road Angel	109
You	115
New Life	117
Notes	126

ACKNOWLEDGEMENTS

The author wishes to gratefully acknowledge the publications in which many of these poems previously appeared: *1997 Anthology of Magazine Verse & Yearbook of American Poetry:* "It Will Be Different This Time:"; *The Bloomington Voice:* "Nakedness"; *Breeze:* "A Place for the Living"; *Celebrating Seventy:* "A Place for the Living," "Earth-Marked Like You"; *divide: journal of literature, arts, and ideas:* "Skin Traveler"; *The Ledge:* "When I Had the American Dream"; *Miners' Ink:* "Beyond Socorro," "Hit Me Again"; *The New York Quarterly:* "The Truth"; *The Pedestal Magazine:* "Frozen Music"; *Returning Women's Handbook:* "This Isn't Your Dream"; *Santa Fe Broadside:* "2000 Women," "Meadowwalk"; *Star Thrower:* "Nocturne," "Self-Portrait," "The Spirit Never Sleep.s," "Stigmata," "This Isn't Your Dream"; *Weber Studies:* "Heritage: The Quest to Identity by a Cherokee Granddaughter"; *Wind:* "It Will Be Different This Time:", "Something Like Church or When A Woman Tries to Change Her Life (A Love Poem)"; *WordWrights!:* "Burning Alone," "Conjuring You," "The Spirit Never Sleep.s". The author recorded "Earth-Marked Like You" for *A Linen Weave of Local Area Poets*, a cassette tape produced by WFHB Radio. The author recorded several of these poems for *Nakedness: Poems of Sensuality and Spirituality*, a compact disc by Cader Idris Productions. Some of these poems were aired on the radio stations WFHB, WFIU, KUNM and on *Area Arts Television* of Bloomington, Indiana.

The author wishes to thank:

Elaine and Sean: for your editorial support and lovingkindness.

Coleman Barks: Rumi poem is from *Birdsong: Rumi, Fifty-three Short Poems translated by Coleman Barks.* MAYPOP, Athens, Georgia, 1993. Used with permission.

Mick Crudge: Words in italics in "Road Angel" are lyrics from songs written by Mick Crudge. Used with permission.

Eric Wallis: *Sun Shining Through* as cover art. Used with permission.

In your light I learn how to love.
In your beauty, how to make poems.
You dance inside my chest,
where no one sees you,
but sometimes I do, and that sight becomes this art.

—Rumi,
translated by Coleman Barks

PREFACE

Suddenly, I began writing poetry.

I would go to sleep at night as a wife, mother and aspiring novelist, then would wake during the night—3:30 or 4 a.m. usually—my soul erupting in song. My soul, something I thought would make her appearance when I died, began a journey—the journey—ahead of the rest of me. My logic, my body, my life was being dragged along by the sheer force of her determination to live freely, uncontained, and the energy of her being was expressed as poetry. Many of the poems in this collection are the beginnings of her life, now *my* life, for while she seemed separate from me on the journey's onset, she and I converged on life's road eventually—she had to stop, turn and wait for me to catch up to join her on her enthusiastic pace, so that she and I could integrate, and our integrity is my poetry.

In the artistic process, an author sometimes must walk the line between creative expression and sensitivity to the cultural and spiritual traditions of others. My intention is to always walk that line with integrity.

When the journey of poetry began for me, I questioned everything about my life, except my deep love and commitment to my children. Beginning a new life in a new city to become a poet and a professor, my children were ever by my side and always in my heart, keeping me "real," for after all, in the midst of incredible spiritual transformation, I still had to make dinner and help with homework ... and listen. As a woman defined by the "rules" of the mid-twentieth century, I found that the basis of my journey to my own identity was often mapped by my relationship to and with men and my desire to understand love. While these poems are based, in varying degrees, on my experiences, they are even more the result of an experience with something greater than my limited views and experiences: they are a soul event.

I believe the words of poetry should create their own music, should speak first to the soul through rhythm, sound devices, and intensity, then later to the mind. It is my hope that listeners and readers of my poetry will hear a "voice" of the poems that relates to a forgotten voice within each of them, a voice that touches their own identities.

—Mary Dezember
Albuquerque, New Mexico

I
AT BAY

When I Had the American Dream

There was a time in my life
When the big event of my day was
Fixing dinner.
I'd start at about 3:30,
With the kids playing outside
Or watching t.v.—content. I'd display
All the ingredients it took to make
A recipe-book meal.
While perfecting pasta writhed,
I'd turn to my chardonnay
And slip into its eyes
As I stirred, sliced and shook.
By the time he came in
The oven pumped hot bread; I
Swirled together a honey-butter spread.
Freeing a beer, he'd lean and kiss me.
Spices peeled the air.
Dinner complete and bottle empty,
I'd call my family to the table;
We'd pray.
As I watched through blurred vision
Everyone I loved more than my own life
Eat, joke and talk about their day,
I was always thinking,
"Dear Lord, how happy I am."

This Isn't Your Dream

When even the bed was feeling right,
and he wasn't there,
she woke to the call. It said:

> "This isn't your dream,
>   So cover your eyes,
>   Or don't come any closer.
>
> I wait."

The next day, lost in her geraniums,
she heard it again. It said:

> "Your window box he hasn't put up
>   Isn't the answer,
>   Or the wallpaper you're saving for,
>   Or the loveseat on order,
>
>   Or the sheets that are holding their breath
>   And yours.
>
>   Listen.
>   Listen."

That night, she listened.

And when she left her bed and went down the hall to meet it, she found it in a closet. It stood like a mummy that never died. Stepping inside, she closed the door. It said:

> "I'm not from him.
>   I'm not even from you.
>   I breathe
>   With something of yours,
>   Somehow
>   Preserving me still
>   By an act from your Ancient, Who
>   Never stops
>   Thinking about you."

Tenderly, she began to unwrap it.

The Truth

I

My friends threw me there. They told me it was a game:
that two friends would grab my arms, and two friends
would grab my legs, and one friend would hold up my
left side and another friend would hold up my right.
It wasn't a game; I knew that. But for once they were
noticing me for something besides my pimples or my A's,
which they despised, and I responded to their attention
and their touch.

And so across the wide field of playground in the town
that circled out from it, a town encircled by fields, a town
defined by blood types my blood could never match,
their fingers chafed and choked my ankles and my wrists
and pinched into my sides—to keep me steady, you
understand, so they wouldn't drop me on my back. Then
there was the boundary, the ditch, and swinging me
forward then back then forward then back (it was about
that time that something happened to my eyes, so when I
looked up at the sway of sky, I saw nothing), they let me
fly, and I punched down into the ditch.

II

At the slumber party, there were games. Seven of us
were invited so that the six could pair off. Each couple
would go to a secret place and talk. Then the six would
regroup in the kitchen. I would wait in the bedroom.
When they called me out to come into the living room,
the object of the game was that I would have to guess
what they talked about and what brand of potato chips

they ate and how many cokes they drank. I didn't like
this, of course; I wasn't stupid, but I was hoping to get
the answers right, and by this, maybe be invited to the
kissing party the next night.

III

On the bus Monday morning, the six called me to come
and sit in the seat in front of the long back bench they
owned. Again I did what they said, but I gained comfort
in the way the boy's ears in front of me stuck out. As
the six giggled about the kissing games, tapping me
on the shoulder and telling me who had kissed who,
describing the mysticism of the bottle, I knew I'd had
enough, but every time I tried to get off my back and
out of the ditch, all I could do was lie there, staring at
sky I believed to be there but just couldn't see, waiting
for someone to notice I hadn't come in from recess, for
anyone to come looking for me.

The Making of Us

My god,
Don't speak,
Just unfold my body
(Across your table will do)
Deliberately,
As if
You love me,
Really love me,
Every crazed crease of me.
Take my nap,
Liberate each holy thread
By your touch in the hush
Of disturbed distance,
The complexity of how
Spirit to air speaks—
The making of us as us complete.
Can you hear this with your fingertips?
I can hear wherever you touch—
Oh I am not just dead cloth
To suit you for your burial,
Though I love to suit you
Before I fall away
As you resurrect in force full-naked.
I am so much more.
Touch again.
Slip your fingertips over me slowly, barely,
Hovering,
With a quiet magnet pull
On the high edge of velvet.
Can you feel now the gazing hands
Of my thousands upon thousands
Of threaded vestal virgins?

They're rising on their toes;
They're climbing each other,
Their hair ruffling readied backs,
Their heightened purple faces calling me! me!
Choose me—
Their fingertips static to yours oh please
Do you see now?
Can you begin to understand
What deliberate can do to them?
They will give their lives—
Any one of them—
For the barest blind glance
From your braille-reading lips.

Now your nose.
Have you ever truly gifted time
In the smell of velvet?
Breathe me how you feel me,
With the promise
That the pull from your lifehalations
Is really only the conception,
The pure suck—
This is my hope
As I age in the prayer
That maybe now you will take me
Right up into you, all the way
Into you,
Through your life-giving nose
And through your greed-harnessed mouth,
Taking scent with her delicious fresh-born children
And the very she of she—
No!—the very Me of Me, yes,
Yes, all the way into you,
Where I will fold in your chest as the dressing

To stop the blood that sheds your heart
So silently
As if
What it wants is to keep you ever unaware
That without me within you,
You are dead,
And I am just your material,
And together we are only lying.

Meadowwalk

Descending makes the sky.
Gray, blue,
Layers of amber hues,
And blood tones.
The pupil seldom perceives
What the heart-master knows:
That we are lost
In this watercolour of souls.

We move about them in this
Corporeal framework, part
Of the cinematic-picture,

But do we ever earn our part?
Everyone is a star.
I'm the one who, if you stare, kills sight—
The frustrated lover, destroying
What I cannot bring back to me,
But then,

So are you.
When we sleep, the camera-eye
Is off us and focuses on our souls,
Who act out ascension. They do it
So convincingly.

They are naturals.
Is there anyone here
To sign them up
On this eternal contract?

When you wake, do you hear the background sound,
A symphony soft in your heart?

And as you rush to your steed on wheels, heavy
-plated with armor,
Invented to project carnality,
Do you glance at the sky
And feel what I see—
The descension?

Why are they here?
To give us a script of rebellion
Or rescue?
To tell us a story of home?

Off book,
I recite to you a soliloquy,
Then you recite one to me.
We never seem to get it right:
Even after our sensual songs,
I feel atmospheric unrest.

We walk through a meadow,
Not speaking now;
It's our day off.

I know what you are thinking:
All would be resolved
If only you could grab me up
Then put me down
And move yourself into me,
Blasting your notion of the life force
And its supposed answers into me.

I point to a light sneaking through
A slip of cloud. I lie when I say
That's you.

The storm that haunts the separated-connected
Bones in my back,
The storm we cannot yet see
As we stroll in this treeless expanse
Of tall green,
I feel it and know that
It is me.

At Bay

I won't love.
This saves me.
It saves me from feeling
Them.
So all I feel now are military terms
That I really don't know about;
But still, you see, the words march
Upside down so their boot bottoms
Make warped impressions
On the inside of my skin,
The underneath part we never consider,
The part that saves me
From being
A skeleton as it sticks to my
Bone, bone, talis-
          bone,
          that a lover of mine
          once tore down to with his ten-fingered
          words, then ripped apart.
          but i survived.
          so i am here now to tell you this:
          joints don't pop
          when you're alive
          and your lover is de-jointing you
          on your wedding night. what they do is
they barely fizz
as he drinks my juice that drips
from them
out of his cupped hands, then complains
that i taste like the weakened champagne
sent from the cheapest of friends.
bones do crack, though,

after he slides them underneath his nails
to rid himself of the grime
then throws them to the hounds
that pant and pace
outside our suite window.
the reek brings them. they
don't go away. speaking of ardor,
i can tell you that it starts out
        like roses, then gets like too many roses
        and carnations and baby's breath
        bound together with ribbons and sentiments,
        so many that the ceiling of the sanctuary
        where you say words like "I will" and "goodbye"
        to someone who won't ever hear you
        seems to be pillared by them,
        and you hold your breath.

    it's true i no longer love.
    i can't risk it.

    and yet,
    there are times i watch
    through the window,
    and i finger the lock.
    they stop.
    our eyes latch.
    love staring me down.
    no motion.
    no sound.

Heritage: The Quest to Identity by a Cherokee Granddaughter
Written when living in Indiana

This may have belonged to one of my ancestors—
This flint arrowhead—
Though I am blonde and pale-eyed . . .

Once I met a woman in a writing class
Who was dark, yes, natively so,
With rough fire-dyed hair,
And a nose that spoke its place,
And eyes that never paled.
She wrote a story
Of how much abuse she had to absorb
At stores and restaurants
West of these parts for being whole,
And I wanted to weave a basket,
Fill it full of stones
That I'd smashed into bevels and points
And of clovers and bark and tiny yellow flowers
I stole from the wild
And carry it all to her,
Dropping my body to her feet
Then pouring my basket out
There at her feet.
Then I wanted to beg her
To close her eyes and to place her hand
On my hair
And to tell me it was thick, rough and black.

But before I even said hello to her,
I quit the class
Simply because her story was so much better than mine.

I have no stories to tell at all
About my part self
Or about my great-grandmother who was full-blooded,
Or about any of my womenfolk who were whole.

I can't even make a sentence,
Because I don't have a word.

But I do have this
That I bought for only seven dollars
At a relic shop
Near my home—
An authentic arrowhead
Plowed up from a cornfield
In these very parts.
I am going to swallow it now,
Gulp it down whole
Without a drink of water.
A grown woman can do that.

I pray
It releases the remedy
To cure that something inside of me
That I can't seem to lance any other way—
This mysterious organ
Sheltered by my heart,
Disguised so well, therefore,
That not even God knows it exists.
It throbs like an abscess.
Streaks of inky poison mercuries from it.
I can taste it grabbing in my throat.
It's frightening.

I think this must be true,
But I really don't know . . .
That these frightening times
When my full-blooded ancestress—
Or any full-blooded woman from
Any time or any place—felt
Her elusiveness throb,
I bet she danced with rhythmic stomping
And chanting and singing—
Everything vital, forgotten and right.

And every time the mystery in her heart
Swelled,
She must have knelt by her fire,
Then jumped,
And surely bolted into the woods
Stalking the scent of moss making love to a stone
In the way it moves up and all over its host,
Wanting it for its very own.
Then clawing the moss off the stone,
She rubbed it, I bet, all over her,
Mashing into her pores
Its musky magic of fearlessly taking for itself
Whatever it wants.

Something Like Church or
When A Woman Tries to Change Her Life (A Love Poem)

she needed more   so yesterday
all and everything she was as a woman
her home decorated
with her mother's antiques her father's paintings
her husband for god's sake
her cat fluffy her dog muffy
her canary jack (he should've flown)
no
their muffy their fluffy their jack
and the acre in which they had sled climbed biked and chased
she carried she carried until she found
a worthy place
then with the fortitude of atlas
she heaved it all
her life her life her life
cracking into a greedy pile
and my god yes she pulled from her apron pocket (mad woman magician)
the matches that had sat in the way-back corner
of the cabinet
(she always knew where everything waited)
struck that match
bared a prayer
and lit it all
and as the flames won oxygen votes then took down heaven
she fell on her breast
as he breathed up the incense
charging his nostrils
and she cried
my babies my god my babies my babies
she heaved again and with the sticky used-up stuff
dripping from her nose and lips

she choked and she moaned my god my god my god my god
what is it I am needing
that is worth all this?
all the rebels chained in her dirt-floored cellar released in triumphant unison
as she hurled herself into the light
and the poets came out of their homes
encircled the fire
and they danced

The Music of You

There is no one who could know   even in part
What it is you are to me
How it really is with my soul
Except maybe for that particular angel   messenger saint
Who devoted his peace casting you into me
As drifts of kindness like
Banners of snowflakes warming the sky in that
Winter that wanted the world   Those
Messages that melted into each other
Creating
What I'll see at my final death
The packed sculpture all that's left
An artifact from you whom
My saint poured out
In softly-sung rations:
The clear stain in my mother's eyes
The way when I stared into them they announced me
Two me's really
But both were you as was
The teacher who called me to his desk
And touched the back of my hand
After my so-called peers had drug me away
At recess and threw me in a ditch
When my father took up the switch
Raising it toward me
But instead hurled it across the room   Now I know
That was you propelling it from his hand
You from the patron who cared for me So this went on
And on You pulsating me in compounded energy
Erect as the best of Sequoia trees
It was there in that forest I called out for you
I wanted to know whom it was I felt

I didn't understand

Loneliness offers the strangest mirror   Compelling and
Tragic but I just had to look just one more look just
One more Maybe that distorted look at me
Is why I stopped way too short in looking for you
And why I curtained myself in nothing
Except the shyest of lace meant only to adorn White
snips
Barely hanging by the hooks of my hips
Framing that view of the beyond where tufts grow wild
Down mysterious clefts
And so in trust and in hope of completeness
This is how I revealed my darkest spot
To the first man I thought I could trust and
He laughed at me
Said I looked stupid ridiculous "Go put your clothes on"

How can I even begin to tell you
What it was like for me as I
Scrambled under the nearest door   a cockroach
Caught in the light How I
Found the commode and let go all his words then dunked
My crusted head held my breath until I couldn't then
Inhaled that crap
Until no other message could flow through me
Life can't pulse from a blood drained heart and after
It was those rancid words not blooded oxygen
That moved my limbs
Directed my walks
As I stumbled over smoldering stumps and under
Dropping charred blocks
I cannot say what it is to be a filled morgue
With all ears deaf

But what I can tell you   my honest love   is that
Years and years later I
Somehow heard
The music of you
And all the bodies cold still and stacked
Within me stirred
And as each moment ripens now in the fresh spring sun
More and more of the dead gently resurrect
And it was You who waited patiently by each
Holding a clawed hand
Kissing a shrunken tear
Whispering a prayer
You moving in dignity from one rotting cocoon to the next
Never giving up on the bodies in me
Transfusing Yourself into me
You the message christening my birth
A lyric I sing in the stresses of breath

II
TRANSFIGURATION

Nocturne

I had forgotten how
Twilight lingers on another's lips
Until the near dawn, how
Clothes fall with the light
From flesh warming in nocturnal rhythms.
I had forgotten how to listen
To the measures of the night
With every part of me.

Today you asked me to your cabin. Cross-
Legged on your bed, I watched you
Make a screen then replace your glass door.
Now, night slants to my body extended and
Cushioned to the hum of yours
On the thin second-hand Arabian carpet
You bought yesterday from a former
Lover. You tell me you no longer love her

As I feel the rough split
Of your hand's healing
Skin move gently
The length of me
And the breath of me
Escapes.
It's almost too bright
As the moon centers her body fully in your door.

Your body shifts also: your back
Shielding us against the prying eyes
Of the heavens. Something flies by
Our breathing screen. Over me, you
Smile, and I lose my hands in your hair.

I ask you to let it grow so that one night soon
I can lose all of me there. For now,
I press my face to your chest, feel you

Breathe, and watch the nocturne.
The moon crosses your frame.
You lie back on the fraying carpet and lift me
Easily over you. We're so quiet
I can hear the communal cry
Of crickets, the far moan of a lone
Owl. I see the fire dance of illumined
Winged artists and the cryptic light of night
That lifts itself out of the earth.
The breeze speaks through trees.
It'll be dawn soon, yet I just can't sleep.
You're awake, too. After your mouth moves
The length of me, you say:
If the night plays
Its soul this way
Why is it
I've always missed it?

Earth-Marked Like You

You ask me to plant with you.
I think it is another one of your
Tests: this one to see
If I am Earthy.
Though I admit I am
A Fire person,
I arrive at your place
Trowel in hand. You, stripped
To the waist and working, stop,
Pull me to you and laugh.
Near the planting bed

You've lit a fire. I can feel
The alchemy of the flames.

I give you
Earth
In a burlap sack, a token
From the deepest place I could find:
A place cleared and
Hollowed for the foundation of a home.
Here is rich red earth,
Earth like clay.
I tell you the story of how
Faith gave a man
Sight

When Christ mixed earth with his Saliva, making Clay,
Then smoothed it onto the man's blind eyes.
I am not God,
So from my bottle of Evian
I pour water onto a handful of this red earth
I've brought as your gift,

For you told me once that from the earth
You draw power.
I mix the clay
In my cupped hand. Using two fingers, I draw
Earth Marks
On your cheeks, then down your nose and across
Your forehead. You close your eyes, and
Lightly,
I smooth the thick earth mix onto your
Eyelids, then generously
Across your shoulders, down
Your arms and up your chest. I move my hands
From you. You tell me you don't need
Sight to see

The fire. Soon, I rest
My hands on you
As I wash the earth from your eyes
With my lips.
Before us, the fire chants
Wood into heady spirits. You open your eyes
And you see
Me
And I am
Naked to the waist and
Earth-marked like you.
You take me up
In your arms and
You take me
Inside
And outside

All our ancestors
Dance as flames; then with you and me, Generations
Burn and kneel and die with the fire...
Melting ourselves back into Earth.

Rapids

This is all that it is: six days from the day we met
I wanted nothing
except you
and a mattress on the floor.
It's still true—I need nothing else,
for now I feel the answer
to all the gaping questions
that had pocked my driest of bodies
down to the grit-pace of my soul:
I had a community of widening fissures,
deserted land mines set-off in a climate-controlled
museum
of parched places, where no one cared enough to visit,
except you,
and for six days you, like a thirsty lion
with probing mirrors for eyes, roamed through me,
and then you left.
The next day it was then, somehow,
the downpour began,
drenching me and filling me
so that not only am I whole now,
complete now,
but white-shocked waters
rush through me
surging me onward into myself—
me turned inside out,
exposed,
my insides naked,
then back again to my now forever just-born self,
slick bare skin—I am
v u l n e r a b l e
in all that is me,

and yet somehow I am dressed
in mystery—the blessed mystery of *how*—
how could I know this?—Intimacy
in its creation,
as the merging of souls,
really, a spiritual thing—
for it has happened,
and I have not known you as body.
My friend,
my body is a dammed prison
to the breaking of these waters,
these towers of waves
that can eat the earth
and make wildflowers out of every dry speck. This
surge,
this surge, charging me
so that all I want now, *all I want now*
is you and me
and any mattress
that can be thrown quick
on the floor.

Self-Portrait

So we've met
What else is there to say?
That I want to unlace my thin ties
And let my dress drift
So that I can stand before you
Just as I am
And we can be lovers
But then my darling those shadows projecting
Upon the wall through the brilliant lens
Of our bodies pressed concave to convex
Would not be ours but theirs
The others we are bound to love   Unless
We keep it too dark to see them   or us
But why only touch   hear   smell   and taste?
Why not also see?
So better that you'd match the wicked oil lamp
I hold in the corner of this bedroom
That offers no bed no nightstand not even a pillow
Or quilt or carpet
Nothing but toxins of the kind
I sweated from my body with marital iron
The toxins I want so maliciously now
That believe it I whittled my wit then cut
And twisted my own valves to make the need and the guilt
Pump more potently So
Here is me waiting for the source
That is you
You with a heart
Too well-routed to ever come here You a collector
Of canonic art who knows better than to steal
From your architect's room
To bring a print of a filled chalice or a

Framed gun (shrined in velvet yet loaded)
Or some other offering Amends against
Furnishing a friend's quick-rent dust-caked fallout corners

      Pieces that would only accentuate the emptiness

It's what I don't see here that scares me
And scares me until I can no longer bar this
Eerie call pacing in me so deep and
It leaps and I release
In quakes from the treacheries of loyalty
And with the fingertip of my free hand
I touch the tip of the tongue of the hungriest of my demons
And trace into the thick
Dust of the wall
The only thing in this room—
A heavy coated figure shadowed without light

The Spirit Never Sleep.s

The Spirit never sleep.s
So when I sleep
She gets her chance.
Sometimes with a quick look
Over her naked silver shoulder
She remembers me,
Then she's off.
More than my pliant shell
And vertebrated thoughts,
She wants you.
Fortunately, she is tethered
By that thick glinting shaft
Anchored in my heart,
Or I'd lose.

She loves you more than her own
Body; she loves you more
Than her own mind. . . .
She tells me this day after day
And
Into the night.
Again,
Into the night
She steps quick,
Her silver dripping thick
Like honey chrysalising.
It's my thick love,
She once told me,
That I want to massage into him,
Starting with his thighs.

Where are you?

Don't you feel her
Chasing the night
As if it held clues
Of you,
As if it were you?

I suppose your nights
Are ones of freedom,
Repose and sex.
I've told her this.
Apparently, she has her
        doubts.
Here,
Morning returns
With only the mourning.

As I wake over the steam
Of my coffee, her finger reaches
Through dark drapes
And makes a vortex
In my cup:
She winces and insists
The feeling is nothing.

Another Dead Child

Again, I carry another cold infant
You left me
And shuffle across the wood of my floors
Looking for something soft of yours
To wrap our child in—
Your cashmere sweater maybe
That you never left here.

I can find nothing,
So I bend my head,
And it moves easily down
Through this little one of ours,
And I wipe my full eyes on his body
That feels like my arm.

I loved this last one
Maybe even more than all the rest
Of our at least a dozen other children,
Whom I loved with the black mark
That writes the letters
That spell the words I love you
That are more true written here
Than they are when they move from your mouth into mine,
Then from my mouth into the oblivion of air
Or your noble head.
This last one I named for you.

Why is it that when you are simply close to me,
Your voice speaking or not,
We conceive?

Of course, it's only within me
That this rightness grows,
Fattened with life by my life
Until it demands
A place in this world of its own.
So, again, alone always without you,

Because you're really never here,
I bear
What you left me.
Birth-streaked and exhausted I stand and give
No thought to anything
But what I have here that we've made,
And with no sleep,
With no food
I stumble in circles
Where dark means light light means dark dark means nothing
Light means nothing nothing means nothing nothing except
Everything for this our child.
I nurse him.
I nuzzle him.
I sing him lullabies using your words—
He understands them better than I. He sleeps.

Then as he reaches for me, just
Before his basic warmth
Could melt my complex heat,
He dies.

So now our little one,
Another son,
I pull to me
Close as I search
For somewhere to lay him—

A tomb
Outside of my cement-blocked body,
      Away from my haunted heart, the womb.

I just can't find the right jewelry box,
Or trinket chest,
Or letter drawer
For this one to rest.

So on the hardest floor of man-nailed wood,
I lie with him tucked
At my breast,
And I curl around him,
And I pull a rug over us;
Then, without understanding,
I loosen my grip
And let the dove fly.

If only I could catch the last fleeting feather.

Please, My Love, don't come
Then leave me again
With nothing
Except what we cannot stop—
The creation left from us together
In your simple slant of time—
Another child who will do
What his father does to me—
Will make me love—
Then will die.

Stigmata

Every word you promised is stigmata:
Oozing wounds of my perpetual death
And salvation.
My heart on its axis turns with the earth;
My mind mocks aridly, never sets;
Your hands on my hands
And my feet and my breast,

Nailing me to a future of unrest.
Arms out, head down, feet swollen,
Above ground.
I thank you and curse you
With every breath of light
And every tasteless night
For the phantasm of you,

Your faceless touch,
The memory of that which saves me and kills me:
You, then your absence, and you
Calling it love—
Voilà—
Attaching me to you
With all the sensitivity of grim iron spikes.

Burning Alone

This—all over me—
the burns of the day,
the eager blisters

barely holding back,
ready to break and cover me:
I wish every one was you.
Pulling with erect knives
of white and blue-edged light and
getting nowhere,

I thought again the only thought that saves my mind:
that maybe someday, someday
you will want me.

Sweet darling,
the truth hides as embers buried in deepened ash
that I stand on as I burn alone, while

you stand on the dusk-cooled shore,
ready to kill clothes,
then stroke in liquid night,

refreshed forever with the someone you choose—
separate tongue-sculpted bodies as one
and soothed.

Conjuring You

I conjure you to come to my bed,
To crawl onto it and smile
And sit next to me
As I lie—
You, unblemished,
And me, perfected—
Neither of us dreams

Of someone else.
I see you bringing me a cup,
And I see how it feels to feel you near, us
Talking over a word. This—
It's a whole life—
This imagining. Yet
Reality weeps:
You love her while I love you.
or
I love him while you love me.
Option C hovers
With a toothless smile
And silver-tipped wings.

Their Last Night

The last time that was
The beginning
Of their final break up—
The blaming and the accusations,
The defensiveness, raised sun-hot voices
And the crying of silent agony,
Attacks on their love—
He had held her all
The night before
In a warm, warm bed
In that mysterious casita in Santa Fe,
His arm over her,
His chest pressed to her back, then
To her side, then
To her chest, and then
Back to her back;
All night, his chest pressed
To different places of her,
His arm always over her,
His hand covering the flesh
That held back the passion
Of her heart beat
His arm over her
gently
gently
gently
Protecting their love.

Recovery

It's seven days since we parted,
seven days in bed
with only Kleenex to complete me,
and I reach for my withered soul
who cowers under the sheet next to me—
she is recovering much more slowly
than I, having had to endure, in addition,
those stampeding stallions
that always trample her
after you love me, then leave.

This time, she cowers from even me.
She wants nothing of my usual consolations.
In fact, I have none to give.

Estranged from her as she grieves and weeps,
I plead to invisibility to know
why is my bed
always one of such agony?

Do you feel any of this?
Is it something that rubs off from the dye
in these stupid paisley sheets?

I'll rip them off and buy white.

I will,
                whenever my soul recovers.

For now, I'll simply hold her.
Maybe that's all she needs
is to not be left alone
in bed.

Maybe I am the one who will stay
and be her friend.

Once In A Lifetime Repeatedly

Every time I see you or simply hear you speak
I have to, once again, get over you.

When I see you or
Simply hear you
It's the intensity of everything love can be
And is
And then, suddenly,
Isn't
All over again.

Within this constant vortex of falling in love,
Being in love, living in love, laughing in love,
Loving in love, being wanted and
Wanting, wanting
Crazy and crazed
As a hurricane bringing peace,
Calm and hot,
Then breaking up
All over again,
I cling to the beauty, the intensity, the passionofpassion,
The Intensity
In fear:
It's too violent.
Seeing you or simply
Hearing you speak
Is
The dark night with
A glorious golden glow—
The full moon shining,
Layers of radiance
Radiating

Radiating

To touch me fully, exactly,
In caves of desire
That have no exit:
I have to turn around and
Leave through the entrance

(I am Master of the Maze).

If I stay inside too long
The torch is ripped from my hand
By some unseen demonmonster
That smashes it against the wall
Drenching me in deepest deepest
Darkness.

For us, my darling,
I stopped crying, finally, one night.

Now, it is simply this:
My blood pulses with tears.

Beyond Socorro

*Socorro is the name of a town in New Mexico
and is the Spanish word for "Help."*

Life is different now
Without you on the fringes.
Hope with his dagger
Has nearly abated.
He takes so long to die:
I tire of watching him.

The landscape in New Mexico
Never speaks of you.
It has other sad tales to tell,
And every moment in this uncanny light
I want to cry.
I never knew you.

The desert mountains are aware of this;
Yet, they don't care.
Their passion is in the sun of dusk:
A flaming bright,
Stunning and dry,
White on white.

Darling, the secrets here are immense.
They are true secrets:
Ones that are never told.
Though I feel them sometimes,
Nearly hear them
When I drive my convertible into the night

Out Hwy. 60
In the direction of the Very Large Array.
It is so dark.
It is so quiet.
It is so out there.
And with my top rolled back,

I am exposed
To something I do not know.
I don't know what.
I can never drive out there
Very far,
Though each time

I pledge to go farther
Next time,
But I never do, because it is
Too quiet,
Too dark,
Too alone.

I feel I am driving right
Into another dimension:

The unknown of the unknown
That must be left
Unknown.

The Motion of the Night

I pull up. *Police,*
I say. You climb in and
You turn
To me.
We leave your friends
To suck stagnant air.
We drive to
We don't know where.

A woman and a man
Together, alone,
Risking our lives
Under an expanse of eyes.
Mystery cloaks my half-
Naked car, and
Into free space
You raise your arms.

The gathering had ended.
I should have driven home
To my fixed life
Instead of into that back avenue
To find you.
I should return you now
To your friends
In their haze.

I should stop this
Machine and
Pitch the stars from your hands and
Pull you to me,
Opening my mouth on yours, and

I should breathe for our lives.
I should let the motion of the night
Explode my soul.

Yet, I keep my face straight.
Except, for this one moment, now.
I glance at you.
Time ignites.
Following the night-drenched
Road,
We drive:
There's no place for the guilty to go.

A Place for the Living

Backed against stone
We sit in midnight,
Restless souls among the ones at rest.
Each relief spells enigma,
Though the depressions name
And date what remains
Mortal.
It's nothing like I imagined.
I'm not at all scared.

I tell you about my mother,
How when I visit her site
I stretch onto the earth
As if I am lying to hold her,
And I move my fingers
Through the grass
Imagining it is her hair.
But it is only grass, I say.
And my mother isn't there.
Every stone appears
In its own light.
I say, *This is a place for the living.*
You whisper, *Let's keep it our secret.*
Something tells me this will be the first
Of our many secrets as I stretch myself
Onto your body
As if it is earth
And move my hands through your hair.

Skin Traveler

Your body is a map of everywhere I want to go.
Yet I can see none of these places are on earth.
With you, I become otherworldly,
A skin traveler,
Visitor to new exciting places, learning of your
Culture,
Your language, tasting your fare, wanting
To share all that makes you, you.

To touch you, though,
I cannot just turn my body toward yours.

I cannot stretch out my leg
And wrap it around yours,
Pulling you to me.

Before I can travel,
I must reach you.

I must reach you, before I
Can taste and touch
And lose my earthy inhibitions
In the joy of your celestial body,
Planetary place
Beyond Planet X

Beyond Pluto
Beyond Sedna
Beyond all I have ever known
That defines and keeps us as bodies,
Physical citizens,
Separate and still

Beyond.

Transfiguration

The broken marble everywhere
Was enough to make her want to dance.
But she couldn't dance
Because of all the people watching.
Well, they weren't people exactly, but
They were kind-of people anyway,
People enough that she'd be
Embarrassed dancing now before them:
So tourist-like, as if she didn't belong here,
Which she didn't, and she did,
She took pictures and roamed through the ruins,
Imagining almost to remembering
What they used to be,
And thanked the gods
That she was the only one here
(Of her kind anyway)
So she had the freedom to be undisturbed.

At first she'd been amazed
That the Forum was so large.
And then she thought:
Of course, it's the Forum. . . .
Fabulous victory parades marched here
And here and here on this mighty road.
She wondered, Whose sandal touched here?
Someone she knew?
Poor Julius or Mark or that Cleopatra!
She knelt to the ground and pressed her ear
To the royal rubble and listened
For the sound of the footstep
That had to be there
If only she could hear it,

For what was really keeping
Her ear from the sound
Of Caesar's shoe? Really, what?

He'd been there
She was there
She'd been there
He was there
More real than her
For this was his place
Not hers
His marble
Carved and laid for his age
Meant for his foot
And she believed that
All the marble knew it
And she knew it
That the marble lived
When they lived
And the spirit
That ties them never dies
It blows still heat
And preserves with the mystic
Quiet and constant Roman sun.

She found with her guidebook
The Temple of Julius Caesar
And rested there, her head leaning
Back on what little was left—
The cement work,
The internal structure of the podium—
Near the altar, his altar,
The Altar of Caesar,
And felt the heat of Rome.

Closing her eyes
And soaking that heat,
Breathing it in,
Her body a sponge,
Needing more heat,
Taking more heat,
Until the sun—
More timeless than that beneath her body—
Moved under her and supported her, then on top,
Covered her,
Covered her,
In layer after layer
Of constancy,
Layers so thick
Bodies could crowd in. . . .

And they did.

And she knew
They were looking at her

She pretended to sleep
But she felt them
Bending over her
Hushed
In wonder
Of who this alienus was
Dressed so strangely
With a black brick hanging on her neck,
A slave from new parts
Brought in by their Caesar?
Or a new goddess maybe
Sent as a warning
From angry Jupiter?

One bent closer
She could hear his voice
Speaking the blessed sound of ancient tongue
And she wished that
Damn it
She'd taken Latin instead of French
Now her heart beat so fast
For she knew she was there
Really there with them
As it was always to be
In a place like this
Where time is the intruder
More than she

She wanted so badly
To open her eyes
To see them over her
In their tunics and leaves
But the sun told her

That sight was forbidden
So she bathed in the scent
Of perfumed ointments
Covering unwashed flesh
The sound of lyric voices
And the feel of the one's
Breath as he hovered
Over her this clever man who breathed
So close to her that now
They were breathing in
The very same eternal air
Somehow she knew that
Somehow he knew that

She wasn't asleep and
He knew her pretense was important
The longer she felt him
The more vital it became
That he not go away
That she not break the spell
By opening her eyes
And she knew he knew
This too.

So near the altar
At Caesar's Temple
Where Mark respeaks the eulogy
For his forever friend forever foe
She and he both prayed
That this moment in time
Would harden like marble
So they could live together forever
In this one deathless moment
Of her insight And his ecstasy

Raising a Dead Body in the Graveyard

A man
Can say anything &
A man will.
So what motivates me now,
Besides foolishness,
To believe you,
Here,
As we walk among the dead?
Maybe it's because you have nothing
To gain in the carnal definitions of being
A man.

You are in love—
Not with me—
With my sister,
My daughter,
The lover in your life.
I love her, too. So
Look at me, here with you,
In the obscurity of twilight. To whom
Am I being true? I say,
All in life is a risk.
Tapping the ground with my toe, I add,

When the risk ends, we are like them.
The moon appears sudden and full,
Riding the gloaming.
It starts to descend to the body
Of the earth. It quickens.
You stare at it. I stare, too. You take
My hand. We are quivering. Our earth
Quakes. I can't believe this is happening.

You say, *I can't believe this.*
I whisper, *It's the apocalypse.*
And here we are, among

Saints.
I move my hand from yours &
With my fingertips
I smooth your hair into place, touching
The skin of your brow only very slightly. Now
I kneel.
I place my hands on the stone.
I absorb its coldness.
The moon starts its ascent.
I press my cheek & my chest to the stone,
& with my face & my breast & my hands,

I feel.
The moon rises.
I hear my pulse in your breath.
The moon is raised.
I turn from the stone to you.
We kneel in night silence framed
By pulsing,
By breathing,
By the awesome
Sweated scent of desire, risk
&
Fear.

Their Ears Hear Only Angels

You rest your head in my lap &
Place your feet on the headstone.
I trace your face &
Your lips, & I think
How I'm kissing you
With my fingertips.
I don't tell you, though,
Because you are my brother,
My son, and such words
Are not in our realm.
I have given up hope

Of ever sharing as a lover,
Of ever knowing what it is to love &
To be loved in return
With the body as much as with the heart.
I am a woman of thirty-nine,
Destined to be this, a virgin priestess:
There's power in celibacy.
I ask how life is for you &
You tell me about your job &
Your friends & your pets.
You don't mention the lover in your life;

I don't ask. I think maybe you feel
You betray her by speaking of her, or
Maybe she has left you to find her life
In a graveyard with someone else.
After a story about your shepherd,
I say that you haven't yet told me about you.
You close your eyes &
I smooth your eyelids with more tenderness

Than anything I have ever done,
Even nursing my child.
You answer that you like being here with me.

I say that you still haven't told me about you,
What you're really thinking,
Feeling. Then I say:
No, don't tell me. Everyone needs
Privacy, some secrets
Of the soul.
Speaking from the lap of your sister,
Of your mother, you say:
That's why we come to this place —
Their ears hear only angels,
And their eyes see only gods.

Cemetery Song

Every marbleized plot
marks a turn from grace
and chastises our desire,
revises our theme.
There are no names here,

only dates of shame
that never culminated love.

No, you say, *it is sacred.*
It is all sacred.

We walk and count
every marker
as if each life
was a word
we said to one another.

The Second Coming

Winter has kept us
Apart.
The first deeply bright day
We meet again
Here,
Where tree roots are buried
With bodies.
It's the same here:
Ornate stones and
Artificial flowers
Make every grave happy, and
Over there, in the grove,
We have midday dusk.
Is it the same with us?

You say how your professors
Are relentless, and
Your friends are relentless, too; yet
Your lover is indifferent, and
You say you think you have terminal illness
Because you just can't face your e-mail.
I say that perhaps my students
Consider me relentless, and
My children are relentless, and
My lover won't leave me alone, and
Perhaps I, too, have terminal illness because
I just can't face my electric male.
I say, *I wish this were a new season.*
Though bright and warming around us,

I feel
You understand me.

You smile in that way that tells me,
Then you smile greater
As you look not at me,
But rather at the monument we lean against.
I've never noticed that, you say,
As your hand outlines a stone snake in relief
Over the name of our host.
Your hair hangs past your shoulders now;
I wish I could've watched it grow and enjoyed the winter.

Today I watch you smile as you touch the snake of death,
and
I think how life always succeeds
In denying me peace, happiness, love.
Your hand and your gaze leave the stone. Finally,
It's my turn.
You look at me for so long I want to look away; I can't.
Then your hand on my face—I close my eyes and move
Into your touch.
With my lips pressed against your palm I can't stop
myself, and
I say, *I love you.*
I keep my eyes closed because I am too old
For love and
You are too young to realize
The knowledge of good and evil waits
Within my limbs.
When I open my eyes,
The sky hasn't darkened;

Neither have you.
Out of the brightness
Something starts to fall.
As if on signal, huge rocks of hail are hurled

From unseen crowds on the clouds,
Stoning me.
My flesh breaks.
With the ease of a father saving his child,
You, unharmed, lift me in your arms and
Run with me to the grove:
Perhaps we'll find sanctuary
In aging limbs and youthful leaves.
You hold me tight against you,
Clasping me up underneath you,

Protecting me from the stones
That do break through.
With my breast to your chest,
I can feel
My heart trying to touch yours.
I can't lift my head because yours shields mine;
You are my cocoon, and
We wait for the pious stone throwers to tire.
When it's over, you straighten, still tightly
Holding me.
The blood soaking your shirt is where
I have wounded you. *My God,* you say,
You are bleeding from the temple
Like there's no tomorrow:
I'll wrap your head with my shirt.
When you're finished, you lift me again.
Pressed against your naked chest,
I pray to bleed to death.
Again, as always when we're together,
Light radiates from somewhere
That's not the sun—
This strange light that binds us and keeps us
Apart.

Your hands tighten beneath my body.
I should say *put me down now* and
You should put me down
Without me having to say it.
You hold me.

With my eyes open,
I hate myself and
I love myself and
I kiss you. Then,
You let me down.
Alone in this grove,
We hear nothing:
Not the world
That must be out there;
Not your lover;
Not your friends;
Not my children;
Not my lover;
Not even each other.
I say, *I'm sorry.*

God, I'm sorry.
I don't speak into my hands
Or into your chest.
I speak facing you. I say,

I am cursed.
Then I say,
Why can't a woman and a man be friends?
Looking past the leaves, I say,
Father, Son or Holy Ghost, where are you?

Why don't you just come out of hiding

And change the world so I can love without pain or guilt?
You lean against a tree.
You say nothing, but your face speaks

A private agony.
Now, the light turns strange, and
The tree you lean on seems to bend into its shadow, and
Its knotted side seems to turn to us resembling weirdly

The shape of a woman.

I look at you. Your eyes are enormous.
You step back. I look at her.
You whisper,
We should meet for coffee like normal people.
With our eyes focused on her, we listen.
The sun intrudes on our vision,
Until all we see is a tree. Yet,
We remain silent, listening: the sun
Intensifies her voice.
I hear her, and I can see from your face that you hear her,
too.
In a voice of feminine assurance and strength, she says:

Children,
Change begins with compassion, forgiveness.
Don't wait for the Second Coming.
The Second Coming waits

Within you.

III
NEW LIFE

It Will Be Different This Time:

I won't separate and bleed
Breath as the corpses of kisses
Dance around my feet, waving their arms
Of crackling red, chanting to metamorphose
My head into a portal through which time
Stops, where I take you and we do everything
Our bodies are moulded to do, and when we return
Not a second has passed; it hasn't really
Happened; no one is hurt. An affair of the heart
Is what those opiated on tradition call it. Ah, but poets
Call it poetry, and actors call it passion or *living
In the moment.* An affair? Though we deny our bodies
And refuse to celebrate what they do best? We are
Cursed.

This time, it will be different:
I have made a pledge on my white breast
To not serve the goddess of desire,
To burn her altar if need be,
For something has got to burn . . .
Better her meats and lies
Than my ecstatic soul.

It's Friday night. You are in your studio,
Rehearsing. I breathe on you,
Though I am in my place across town. This is
Art.

The Healer

You ask nothing of me,
Even as you sit on the edge
Of the bed

My mother left me.

Mom asked nothing of her health
Professionals or of me,
Even as we watched her vanish

Into hospital sheets.

She asked nothing
As each body and soul in medical degrees
Approached the bed to check on her

Deterioration.

Rather, my mother, with her nothing-left arm,
Reached for the one nearest her,
And she prayed aloud for that person's secret need.

I don't remember her words, still

I do remember this:
Every person left her room
Shaken.

I know what they were wondering—

I was wondering, too.
How could this quietly suffering woman
Pray for those pains she could not know?

It was nothing less than the miracles

That had kept her
Alive for twenty-six years.
A terminal disease for twenty-six years,

And most of that time,

You would never know.
I was twenty-eight during those last days,
When all I saw and heard was

A woman at prayer,
As if I'd stumbled somehow into
Her most sacred space. Humbled,
I knew the ache of truth.

I saw

The woman in transition—her spirit

Expanding from her melting body.
I remember her crying for the suffering
Of the aide who had left the guard

Rail down. That night, I

Had gone home to sleep.
In a midnight state, Mom dreamed
She was home

And left her bed

To, I don't know, maybe brew a cup of tea,
And the bully disease shoved her tiny body
To the floor, then snapped her hip.

Nothing will heal now, Dr.
Said,
And they stopped feeding her and
She lay stuck flat on her back feeling

Her flesh break into blood

Until she fused with the sheet. I sat by
That bed as I sit
In a chair by this bed now, with

You on the edge,

And, like my mother,
You ask nothing of me.
Unaware of my orphan's story, you

Are a man who somehow knows

How to touch those memories
We hide in our bodies.
Before us, through the sunlit lace

At my window, I can see
The snow gently melt.
You reach for me.
From this hard wood chair, you lift me.

You cradle me in your lap,

Brace me calmly against your chest, then
Bravely
And carefully,

You rock me.

Midnight, December 25th: Divine Outlaws

Skulls watch us.
With vision
Hollow, blank,
They stare at you and me
Waiting, framed
Together in the fire
Light.

It's your decor.

Your depth is a core
Of radiation
Wilder than our fire—
What I call charisma,
Though you, coughing, say:
No, sister, it's the
Physics
Of dying to ashes.

Can't you see

Even in this bright night
That gifts
To those who don't use them
Must be given to another?

There is no loss in this,

For it is spiritual
Multiplication, and
It will shake our lives
As we shed pain like shards

Falling from our souls upon your
Wood
Floor
Shattering.

Within my body,

I feel this call; yet,
I wish we could hear
What is happening and
You'd hold me in the mind-
Breaking sound of healing

Until it all ends.

Then the skulls at long last
Will grow eyes and
Upon us will
Smile.

Life Wish: The Art of Discernment

When a new voice speaks to you,
Saying:
> *Do not fear death;*
> *It is just another form of life;*
> *Now, come to me;*
Say back to it:
> *That's hogwash.*
Really—
Hogwash. For as the man
Who dashed his daily and nightly bruised body

Against tombstones,
Bleeding on the graves there,
Pleading to be released there,
Trying to break his body open
To set his spirit free—
No—he didn't fear death.
He feared the life that holds the body
And hosted the voices that enter
And desperately try to suck it.
And on that desert day when

The other
Stepped into this place of tombs
And spoke the word,
The dashing man stopped bashing himself; he
Sat and cooled in the shadow of the other—
The other bending to him, tending to him—
And smiled
For the first time in years.
And down the hill
Hogs dashed

Into the sea
Fearlessly washing themselves there:
Sea washing them;
Sea washing over them;
An ocean of hog washing;
Hogs sucking the sea—
Hogwash outside then inside—
Hogwashing themselves
To death
And into their never beyond.

Shiggaion

If someone had grabbed Sylvia's end
out of that flat
away from the cubicle of haunted thoughts
and the perpetual thirsts
of blossoming luvs
and threw her into a café
for just a few hours everyday, then told her
to serve burgers to crazed ravenous customers, then
maybe...

I was getting weird,
pouring out my flowing soul
at 4 a.m. as my children slept.
I didn't know about the dry-mouthed dead
lurking to lap me up.
They told me they loved me.
I started to believe them.
Isolation, soul-letting and rejection
from corporal lovers
can make you receptive
to ever-departed pseudo-seducers.

Mine disguised themselves
in famous names
of lauded artists
and cheered me on
as they watched me write barely-balanced
on the lip of their abyss.

My soul like a mother cried.

That wasn't the part of her I wanted to hear.

Instead, as if her voice was a commodity,
I sucked it in song
and blackened it on paper.

Why didn't I protect her
like I do my daughter
and my son?

Too busy translating her language,
I didn't notice
how she was suddenly in adolescence
(or mid-life)
responding too quickly to her peer-group
from the wrong side of the tracks.

She had not yet learned
discernment.
Nor had I.

She struggled against awkwardness
while she grew too fast for her body:
she tried to shrug me off.

So there I was,
a woman on the patio of a café
writing irregular songs of the soul,
as I shrugged my shoulders
again and again because
my spirit wanted out.

Out of the edge of my detachment,
I could sense the server,
who very basically served burgers
to the very basically hungry.

Meanwhile,
loving my soul for her honesty
and her loyalty,
I continued to write
on the lip of the abyss.
Those gaseous voices churned deep within it
and rose up to me.

Who was the hungriest?

From the Realm of the Real Poets,
comprised of those who in truth
do love me
and want me to have life
as much now
here
as later,
rose the greatest of these.
He (of the sHe) grabbed my end
out of my flat,
away from my roses, my tulips,
and threw me back
again and again
into this café
and whispered one day beneath the ear to the owner
to come over to my table and,
at a wage no sane poet could refuse,
offer me the job
of serving
as manager
over the servers.

Hit Me Again

Too much youth
is like too much wine—
it makes you think you have powers
beyond what you have.
Rimbaud (clever soul) told me this,
yet maybe in my even saying such a thing
I speak like a drunkard
and write even worse
and have not the talent
or not nearly the vitality
my cohort had who stopped writing at 19,
then died at 37,
the age I began.
So maybe all I have is
audacity
and harvested farmlands of pain
and the tatooing discomfort
of trying to tell you this,
and hoping that in doing so
I'll get some relief,
so I call it acupuncture.
Now,
I've given up wine
and youth gave up me
and people like mirrors were once criminals
until I learned the way of looking through their eyes
and understood finally their function
is to reflect light—
not my image
or my judgment.

2000 Women

2000 women camped on the banks of the river that nourished the nation. They wove their hair into brown and gold and black and red halos, singing lullabies to the ways of their mothers. Raising their palms to the sun, they caught fire, balancing it as air slightly above them, then cleansed and warmed themselves in its heat and its light as they dropped their hands and let it melt upon them as golden lotion.

2000 women built homes on the banks of the river that flowed through the heart of their nation. They furnished their homes with honey candles and cinnamon incense, herb-laced windows, and all tables were round. When men came from cities or woods or deserts, 2000 women responded only to desire tempered by gentleness and generosity. On this, 2000 women would not compromise. And this was their love.

When the men slept in rose petal beds, 2000 women would go to their children's rooms, lift them in their dreams, and carry them to the banks of the river. As the men slept in the homes and the children slept in their mothers' arms, 2000 women raised their voices to the moon and caught its fire, balancing it as air slightly above them: They sang moonfire.

Under the moonfire of the singing mothers, the women with no children in their arms danced. They danced. With moonfire drenching them, they danced. Sweating with dance, they tenderly took the children from the mothers and cradled them as if they were their own. Then the mothers danced. With moonfire drenching them and in the honeysuckle breath of their sleeping children, the mothers danced. After the dance, and carefully taking the children from the arms of their sisters, the mothers replaced their new ones in their beds. Leaving their homes again, the mothers returned to their patient sisters.

2000 women stood on the banks of the river
that nourished the nation, and at the hour that
is not night
yet
is not day,
2000 women raised their magnetic hands
and in unison
pulled the sun out of hiding,
lifting it slowly,
dispelling the darkness
with the magic of passion:

Female Energy

Conscious Pilate

With a final strip of authority,
one of the six tugged tight
the linen around the facial eyes
of the seventh, then spun him.
The seventh obeyed, moving
concentrically; the sound and the feel
of the whip notching his side was real.
"Who holds the whip, Prophet?"
Laughter. Pass the whip.
"Who holds the whip, now, Seer?
Name his name."
The flit and the dart of robes
about the alabaster walls
was the revelation of her, a death's
head moth with an unpowdered heart,
against the white empty night.
This was more than an easy headache
or a needed nightmare that shook her
from her rest and sent her searing
about the edges of the scene.
Her skull cracking in and out
in an explosion of the answer,
she ran full to the man
whose place in time granted
him the grain of power. "Have mercy
on that one," she cried, falling
and writhing at his feet. Pulling
to her mouth close and whispering
to the toes that she'd once
sucked, she pleaded, "I have
had a dream. My head burns.
Let him be. Let him be."
Lifting his foot, he shrugged
her off and said in a clear,
monosyllabic tone, "Go."
Daggers of air marauded her body,

raped her soul as she looked
from this man to that man to
this man to that. "Listen to me.
Listen to me," she said.
He kicked her.
Wings wet with tar, she left
the scene, speaking bright:

```
                          "I fell to
                          the feet of
                  w       the wrong
                  h       king. . .and       w
                  a       the wrong          h
                  t       husband."          a
                  i       Words like         t
                  s       fire sprang        i
                  t       in pillars;        s
        w         r       a crisp            t
        h         u       stonehenge         r
        a         t       thinned out        u
        t         h       of time en-        t
        i                 circled the        h
        s                 impenetrable
        t                 rite. . .
        r                                    w
        u         w                          h
        t         h                 w        a
        h         a                 h        t
                  t                 a        i
                  i                 t        s
                  s                 i        t
                  t                 s        r
                  r                 t        u
                  u                 r        t
                  t                 u        h
                  h                 t
                                    h
```

100

Don't Touch Me, For I Must Leave You Again, This Time, Forever

Please, Mary, don't touch me.
The separation these last days
And nights
Has been too much
Pain.
Tangible colors
Of leaves and stone and earth
And you
Became a memory
Of a firm loveliness
And completion:
The pull from the blinding light of beauty
To a basic place
Elemental and pure
The spirit contained
And concentrated,
Reverberating the walls
Of the body,
Attracting the waves of the All
And internalizing them
Into one compact universe
Called me,
Called you.
If you touch me, Mary,
I might explode:
For we are magnetized stars
That *should* collide
Transforming two distinct matters
Into one electric energy.
We were apart only two days and nights,
And I missed as forever your smile,

The aura of your lips,
And now I see you again—
You are so close
I can feel the warmth of your humanity.
I want to feel human again.
Mary, I want to feel.
I want to touch your hand and your face,
Pull you close, my dearest friend,
For what pleased my soul here
Was the pleasure of friends, who they *are*,
And here they are bodies, the wells of souls:
It is the physical of physics.
In fact, there is no loss in transformation.
Yet, in truth,
I felt the greatest loss
That ripped me open into bleeding pieces within my tomb,
My Hell,
My God, to be held by another person, the body of a friend,
Just once more,
To feel the human form,
To just be touched.

What is this that resurrects my life and brings me back
To the memory of myself?

My Mary,
Don't touch me.
If you do,

I'll stay.

The Chosen

Last night
As you traced my face
      with your fingertips,
           gracefully as a night prayer,

I wanted to tell you
How your gentle touch
      moves through me
           beyond the shy depths of flesh,

And I wanted to say
How a kingdom now
      thrives within me,
           a kingdom you've awakened.

Though I wanted to tell you this,
I respected your silence
      and reflected
           your silence

For you and I know without speaking
That there are times
      when even our whispers
           would be intruders

On the stillness we recognize
As the voice of God.
      My darling,
           I stand before you

And say the words "I will,"
And I mean this—

       I will love you
             for I am the King's heir

Christ's representative,
His embodiment Somehow, sired to love you,
      and in the best way that Christ
           Himself can smooth your brow

And share with you His love
I have been chosen
      to touch you
           in the quiet.

Nakedness

If my body could fall away
and your body could fall away,
then we could love in the way
I think love was really meant.

Nakedness is not our clothes falling away,
but our bodies, our bodies flung off finally,
freeing us finally,
to suck each other entirely
together,
all of us together
clothed bodies flung everywhere
& us loving us loving us
as pulsating pulsating
waves & suns
rising so high to still the heat
heating so low to start the rise

Frozen Music

I don't know if I can write anything...

Mostly I want to be quiet
During this time.
Not be even a poet.

Mostly be not a poet.

Too many emotions to catalogue or articulate
Or hear
Or feel.

It is the day after
And I am so wiped out
I just want to be home,
Reflective,
Holding in my heart those still trapped,
With the others
Dead,
Crying,
Thankful my loved ones are alive. . . .

Instead I drive 85 miles
To teach the arts to youthful techies
Whose hearts may be buried in the architecture
Of the supposed future,
And it is useless, I think, to help dig them out:

I must try.
Even if it means my life.
I must try.

It's the human way.

So I present the architecture of the Colosseum,
And my voice wavers when I tell them

That during the celebration of its dedication
2000 men and 9000 animals were killed.

And then I say that architecture is for art and for beauty,
Yet more than that,
Architecture is for life,
Protection,
Today, from the elements,
Yesterday, from the enemies,
Moats and drawbridges and walls and walls and walls.
Now, suddenly,
Today is Yesterday:
There can never be enough fortresses.

Do we never progress?

I think of my children, of my students,
I think of
Everyone,
And I think to myself—
As my students wait for me to speak—
I think,
Please, Someone, keep us safe.

I take a breath and say,

"Architecture is not for killing.
It defines space for sanctuary; it is
'Frozen music,' Frank Lloyd Wright said,
Describing its composition, the rhythm of its design,
Though I think it can also mean that
Architecture
Transports us and keeps us
Safe in that haven
so we can work and play and love.

Architecture is for love.
People are for love."

I am silent.

We are all silent.

In the silence—
The darkened space—
We look at the only light in the room,
A computer-projected image of the classical ruin,
Yet I know
Each of us sees other ruins—

Those of world trade—

Innocent lives for innocent lives.

I check my watch.
There is time remaining.

I've done what I can behind these walls
For today, and maybe even something
For tomorrow.
I open the blind.
Sunlight overpowers the feeble projected image.
We blink and shield our eyes.
I switch off the computer and say,

"Be kind.
That is all."

I drive, 85 miles, home
To my children—
Our children
Waiting.

Road Angel

Angels have no wings.
They are not separate from us.
I have known two.
The first I cannot speak of:

I have sworn an oath.

The second . . .
Well, the second sings road songs.
A minstrel, you might say,
Though he prefers troubadour—
You've seen such Renaissance angels
In paintings,
Except they play a lute or a lyre.
A contemporary wandering angel who sings
Songs of the road needs a guitar—
I ask you, what is a guitar if not the machine-gun rock-on
Wedding of lute and lyre?

He says,
"It is not easy making your place
as a messenger of peace.
Wings are too obvious, noticeably strained,
And so are some songs:
The '80s and the '90s were extremely tough
For getting the good word out."

He tells me that to live here
Angels, too, live by trial
And error
And error . . .
And error.

Though he says his days singing lead
In a London-based punk band were
Good.

These days, he strums mostly mellow
At the plaza Starbucks in Santa Fe,
Singing of *joy*
And its other side,
Of *painted ships on painted seas*,
And the images that make us
And the illusions that scatter us;
"Be together; be at peace,"
he would have sung
If he'd been here in the early '70s,
For this angel has a message:
Love one another.

You have heard this before?

Today is Easter,
And I think if Easter means only one thing,
It is this:
Love one another.

My friend the angel sings Easter
Along Route 66. He says,

"Easter is a road song—
It returns each year to resurrect
The love we sacrifice."

In coffee houses and pizza pubs and funky
Restaurants across the U.S., this angel sings,
There are no foreigners.

Listeners listen.

He adds,
So bring the harvest home.

Making we wonder, can we?
Can we plant, nurture, let grow, harvest,
And share in the bounty of love?

The angels I have known
Have no wings—
My friend the Road Angel

Says that if he did, he would request those
Of the colorful nearly-extinct Micronesian Kingfisher.
I say, "Purple-blue wings with cinnamon lining."
I add, "And eyes masked in deep-green."
He plays a cord, smiles, then sings:
The other side of within
Is waiting to begin.

He bows his head over the guitar, and a crow
Feather braided into his hair falls in front
Of his hands;
Gently, I push his braid behind him
So the feather lies at his back.

"Or maybe," he says, "I would have the wings of the abundant crow."
I say, "Deep blue-black as the path to the supernatural
Where the sacred methods to peace await."

Only moments ago, during song when in a basement coffee house,
Around him a white light, wide
With ragged edges,

Encircled his entire body.
At first I thought tears were trapped in my contacts,
Blurring the florescent light,
Though I realized almost instantly that while his song was moving,
I wasn't crying
And there was no florescent light.
The truth be told, in this basement coffee house
There were few sources of light at all,
Just him.
I was transported, watching the wide circle of light
Vibrate about him
Feeling the rhythm
Hearing the melody
Breathing the harmony
Of peace.

I thought,
In Renaissance art,
I bet this circle of light was painted
Smaller and only about the head—
Why not larger, the way I see it?

After his gig, I asked him about this:
He smiled and said, "Well, Love,
How about a cup of tea?
Earl Grey? Or better, something herbal? Will that do?"

In the room where he stays when he's not on the road
And sleeping in his car,
I watched him pour,
And as the water steamed up from the cup,
Rising in its new form,
He said,

"Angels have no halos.

They are not separate from us.
They have light.
We have light.
When we finally get it,
What we know is
We all have light."

Nodding, I said,
"My mother used to say,
'We all walk in the light we are given.'"

Handing me my cup, he sipped from his.
I wanted his cup, but I took mine.
Gifts are always warm; the best ones are hot.
A little at a time.
A little at a time.
I sipped.
He said, "It is all light."

"It is all light," he said again
The next morning
After he stopped just long enough to say goodbye
And to kiss lightly each of my eyelids,
And when I opened them

All I could see
Was him
Disappearing
In his '67 Thunderbird.

Angels have no wings.
Still, they must move.
This is their purpose—
To fly with a message

For those who are earthbound,
A vital message:
One that can take root, grow, then expand in our hearts,
And expand and expand,
Breaking the bounds of our beautiful earth pace,
And explode right through us, behind us, no longer a chrysalis,
We are its harvest,
As white light,
Ragged on the edges, like feathers,
Encircling us,
So that if you could see it
This message would look curved, wide, long, full
Like wings
That arch above our heads,
Flow along our bodies, cascading
In white white,
Not forgetting
To touch earth.

You

Hope jettisons:
I had paid a fevered price
Hoping to keep
Hope alive. Then it came to
Me or her, so
I destroyed her. I simply
Drove a stake through her heart
And buried her in the depths
Of my soul.

And now
You.
And now Hope revives wildly, erupting from my body,
Lightening me, attesting to Me.

As white light, she and
I move smoothly through
Dark corridors and
Dank tunnels.

The haunting loves who craftily try
To corner me, beat me, and drag me
To their tombs

Are now unfit to do anything
Except to flow with my flow. I'm so sleek,
Even their voices hush.
They can't even warn me.

I am
Ecstatic and horrified to see
That they no longer quiver greedily above me. I

Worry they are only lost in and not vanquished by
The vortex of Hope
Created by the layered, rushing, heating and cooling images of
Your smile, Your eyes, Your
Words.
You, newborn swords of incendiary light,
Why did you ignite Hope and arouse my
Incandescent breast? It can't be true.
A man with innocence seems impossible.
Love seems impossible.

Yet here You are.

Yet You are here.

This poem supposes that before birth, we were who we are, living a spiritual life in a spiritual realm that we will return to at death, and is positioned at the moment of such realization, after a poetry reading, when someone begins seeing her former life—it is a long poem that moves from the present to the pre-life past then back to the present.

New Life

  After reading Dante Alighieri's *La Vita Nuova*

 The year 2000 marks the 700th anniversary of Dante's walk
  through fire in Purgatory to meet Beatrice and their journey
together into Paradise, of which he writes in the Divine Comedy.

circa 1999:

Until we know,
Until some miraculous Saint
Walks up

And says,
And why are you here?
And looks all the way through you

Until you are naked before him
In the most beautiful of ways,
We don't know

 And society dictates.

Handing you his glass of wine,
He takes from you the book you hold out to him.
Then, for a moment, this Saint averts his eyes

From you to the book, his book of magic words.
In it, he writes his name and yours.
You return his glass,

Thirsting for more.

He has spoken to you in an arcane language,
And he has seen through you
All the way to pre-memory.

You know him in a way
You've never known
Anyone or any moment before,

And, yet, you just met.

He is the Poet: the Medicine Man, the Muse Master, the Mirror,
Somehow oddly,
He is You.

Literature now has meaning you realize.

Realize: He has eyes so real; He is the Seer
Who has uncovered every mystery of you,
And still, it is all mysterious, for in this kind of life

Mystery forever increases, procreating
Herself in lasting, enveloping,
Accepting vaginal and womb ways.

And you know this type of meeting is not just for Beatrice and Dante.

When the literary event ends
You and he must part,
Yet the Poet commands every moment.

That night you begin having visions
Of your life before Corporeality:

        You were a Priestess in the Sphere of the Grand Mother,

And you were loved
By an entire village
Of glowing forms,

Persons who lived in silvery green-leafed huts.
At night, when they turned their faces up towards yours,
You blessed them each,

Some with a touch,
Some with a kiss,
Some with a look

As deep as the Poet the Shaman had looked at you
After that long ago, long to be
Poetry reading that happened only today.

Then, when your charges are asleep,
You run on feet that know no earth
To a hill where the Poet waits.

He is your one true incomparable love.
There has never been anything like this on earth:
You love him and he loves you.

Your loving is purely and wholly and holy and completely
Erotic and chaste,
And you learn and honor and bless

Your glowing bodies with tongues and lips
And fingertips and flesh that is pulsing heat
Merging in a naturalness beyond nature.

His back against the hill, your back along his torso,
Breathing hushed harmony,
You look through tears at the same stars

You will see from earth

When you leave this place.
Together you speak of your destination and destinies,
Your missions that must be:

For the world needs poets.

You cry at the thought of your separation
From this life,
This place,

But mostly you cry at the inevitability of your separation
From him—the One you love,
The One who is more you than you.

You part and you know you will see each other again,
Tomorrow night,
Until that day of departure came,

And you lost each other in the Carnal Quest,

And you even lost your memory,

Until now.

And now, have you lost your mind?
You wonder as you wake, knowing the life
You've imagined is more real

Than this life you are living.

Nothing changes except intensifies
As this next day progresses,
And you see him again that evening, because

(Thank God for endowments)

There is another poetry reading.

And it is the same except richer
When he looks at you.
You need not even speak of it,

For you know he knows,
And your soul is leaping,
The soul you didn't even know you had,

The one that was supposed to suddenly surface at death:
She is here.
She dances.

Standing now between you and the Poet, she faces you and says:
You did your best to kill me—
You and your society. And you did. You buried me alive,

Smothered me, killed me, though

I am resurrected.

And you can never overpower me again.
Moreover, you will never do anything again without looking through me,
For here I stand forever before you.

And through your soul you see your Saint:

He is even more magnificent.

It is time. Your Saint must go home, write more poetry,
You can't go with him.
The illness that follows is insanity.
You suffer from Supreme Paranoia,
For all the poets who have come before you
Are watching you—they are here for you!—

No one on earth cares about you: they don't even notice,
But everyone in Heaven watches you. What's more,

They are your advocates, they chant for you!

They want you to join them as a literary name,
And you've never wanted anything more,
Except to rejoin with your love.

But he has gone; he has predetermined earthly duties

Of which you are not a part.

So alone you hold on—to what?
Alone.
So alone.

You can tell no one,
For they would ostracize you in white and straight jackets,
Or shock treatments?—though if they tried, you are so charged

You would blow the machine to kingdom come.

You are out there,
Everywhere,
A live circuit,

An open channel,
Electromagnetically
Catching every wave,

Hearing every voice,
Seeing every vision
Beyond the veil

Into the other worlds.

You are in the wilderness,
Caught in the middle of a mad, living, flaming, craggy current
And you have no devices.

There is nothing you can do,
Except flow with the wildness
And pray that during this

You don't die.

There is nothing to hold onto;
Nothing
Except your faith.

And you believe
That all is sacred,
Even this is sacred

Though it feels like hell,

And visions and voices are not just for Dante —

Though you wish to God they were —
Because this really seems insane,
Yet you are more healthy than you've ever been before,

And Rimbaud says, *Just believe, it is all God, what I*
Could have done after age 37 if only I understood the
Quintessence of faith;

And Sylvia says, *It's not worth it, give up poetry*
If it leads you to this, to where I am now, where I went
When my babies slept in the next room;

And the benevolent voices of long gone still here poets say,

We believe in you,

And the other voices say,
It is your body that is keeping you down. Throw it off
And join us. The best poetry is written here.

And as badly as you want to be a poet,
And as badly as you to want to return to your before afterlife,
And as badly as you are suffering and you cannot take any more,

Can not take any more   Can not take any more

Suffering,
And your body has become so heavy,

So heavy,

You say to them:

"No."

You say:
"I accept this life,
No matter what that means.

If I am never to be a poet,
Then I am never to be a poet.
This moment is the only truth I know,

And at this moment, I am more than rhythm and words and glowing soul.
I am Flesh.
I am Body.

I am Lips and Neck and Nipples and Navel and Buttocks and Clitoris and Lips
I am
Heart and Blood and Lungs
I am Breath

Embodied."

After many more harrowing months,
Some kind of nonexistent yet real

Savior of Passion pulls you with graceful force

From the craggy current, the vortex of voices,
And dries your body with lilac,
Clover, jasmine

And with his long, soft halo of hair.

Now you know that never loving with the body is just for Beatrice
    and Dante.

So now?

All you have is faith.

NOTES

"Don't Touch Me, For I Must Leave You Again, This Time, Forever" is a dramatic monologue in the voice of Jesus upon resurrection speaking to Mary outside his tomb. (Refer to New Testament in the Bible, King James Version, John 20:17).

"The Chosen" was written for and read at the marriage of Kelli and Chad.

"Frozen Music": Information about the number of men and animals killed during the dedication of the Colosseum is from *Rome of the Caesars* by Leonardo B. Dal Maso, Bonechi-Edizioni «Il Turismo», 1974, page 67, which states: "The writer Dion Cassius relates that during these festivities 9000 wild beasts were killed and some 2000 gladiators lost their lives."

"Road Angel": Idea for the description of the crow feather is from information about the crow's eye in *Medicine Cards: The Discovery of Power Through the Ways of Animals*, by Jamie Sams & David Carson, Illustrated by Angela C. Werneke, Bear & Company, Santa Fe, New Mexico, 1988, page 133: "If you look deeply into Crow's eye, you will have found the gateway to the supernatural." Information for the description of the Micronesian Kingfisher is from the Lincoln Park Zoo website, http://www.lpzoo.com/animals/FACTS/birds/micro_kingfisher.html.

www.ingramcontent.com/pod-product-compliance
Lightning Source LLC
Chambersburg PA
CBHW031139090426
42738CB00008B/1146